ALFRED UHRY

DRIVING MISS DAISY

W0195935

Cornelsen

Alfred Uhry
Driving Miss Daisy

Herausgegeben von
Ursula Küppers
Ingrid Ross

Verlagsredaktion: Neil Porter

Umschlagillustration: © Interfoto, München

Copyright © 1986, 1987 by Alfred Uhry.
Used by permission of Flora Roberts, Inc.

Driving Miss Daisy was first produced Off-Broadway by
Playwrights Horizons, New York City in 1987.
It was subsequently produced by Jane Harmon / Nina Keneally, Ivy
Properties Ltd. / Richard Frankel, Gene Wolsh / Alan M. Shore
and Susan S. Myerberg in association with Playwrights
Horizons Off-Broadway in 1987.

 http://www.cornelsen.de

1. Auflage € Druck 8 7 6 5 Jahr 08 07 06 05

Alle Drucke dieser Auflage sind inhaltlich unverändert und können
im Unterricht nebeneinander verwendet werden.

© 1998 Cornelsen Verlag, Berlin

Druck: CS-Druck CornelsenStürtz, Berlin

ISBN 3-464-06325-9

Bestellnummer 63259

Gedruckt auf säurefreiem Papier, umweltschonend hergestellt aus chlorfrei gebleichten Faserstoffen.

CONTENTS

There was a real Miss Daisy. She was a friend of my grandmother's in Atlanta, back in the forties when I was a child. She was a "maiden lady" as we called it then, the last of a big family, and she lived in what I remember as a spooky old Victorian house. There was Hoke, too. He was the sometime bartender at our German-Jewish country club, and I believe, he supplemented his income by bartending at private parties around town. And Boolie ... well, I didn't really know him, but he was the brother of my dear Aunt Marjorie's friend Rosalie. They were real people, all right, but I have used only their names in creating the three characters in Driving Miss Daisy. I wanted to use names that seemed particular to the Atlanta which I grew up in. The actual characters, though, are made of little bits and pieces of my childhood. Quite a bit of my grandmother, Lena Guthman Fox, and her four older sisters have gone into Miss Daisy herself. And I guess my mother, Alene Fox Uhry, is there too. Hoke is based on my grandmother's chauffeur, Will Coleman, but also on Bill and Riley and Marvin and Pete and other black chauffeurs I knew in those days. And Boolie is so many pieces of so many men I know (including me, I suppose) that it would be hard for me to say what exactly comes from what.

I find that there is unusual interest in my offstage character Florine, Boolie's wife. Many people have said (by mail or person) that they know Florine, she is their aunt, their cousin, their old friend from home, etc., etc., etc., and who was she really? I will never tell.

When I wrote this play I never dreamed I would be writing an introduction to it because I never thought it would get this far. The original schedule was a five-week run at Playwrights Horizon, a New York nonprofit theatre, in the spring of 1987, and I made sure various family members from Atlanta would get to town during that period. The theatre seated seventy-four people. Just the right size, I thought, for a little play that could surely have appeal only to me, my family, and a few other southerners. To my amazement, the appeal was much wider. When the five weeks was up, the engagement was extended for another five weeks, and by then the demand for tickets was so great that we had to move to a bigger theatre.

Flash forward a year and a half. Now there are several companies playing and many more productions planned in all parts of the world. I am in the process of writing the screenplay. I have won the Pulitzer Prize. Even as I write these words they seem unbelievable to me. When I wonder how all this happened (which I do a lot!) I can only come up with one answer. I wrote what I knew to be the truth and people have recognized it as such.

Alfred Uhry

Abbreviations

abbr.	abbreviation	joc.	jocular
AE	American English	n.	noun
BE	British English	pron.	pronunciation
derog.	derogatory	sb.	somebody
fml.	formal	sl.	slang
infml.	informal	sth.	something
jdn.	jemanden		

Characters
Daisy Werthan · a widow (age 72–97)
Hoke Coleburn · her chauffeur (age 60–85)
Boolie Werthan · her son (age 40–65)

Time and Place
This play takes place from 1948 to 1973, mostly in Atlanta, Georgia.
There are many locales. The scenery is meant to be simple and
evocative. The action shifts frequently and, I hope, fluidly.

Driving Miss Daisy was first produced Off Broadway by
Playwrights Horizons in 1987.

ALFRED UHRY

DRIVING MISS DAISY

In the dark we hear a car ignition turn on, and then a horrible
crash. Bangs and booms and wood splintering. When the noise is
very loud, it stops suddenly and the lights come up on Daisy
Werthan's living room, or a portion thereof. Daisy, age 72, is
5 *wearing a summer dress and high heeled shoes. Her hair, her*
clothes, her walk, everything about her suggests bristle and
feistiness and high energy. She appears to be in excellent health.
Her son, Boolie Werthan, 40, is a businessman, Junior Chamber
of Commerce style. He has a strong, capable air. The Werthans
10 *are Jewish, but they have strong Atlanta accents.*

DAISY: No!
BOOLIE: Mama!
DAISY: No!
BOOLIE: Mama!
15 DAISY I said no, Boolie, and that's the end of it.
BOOLIE: It's a miracle you're not laying in Emory Hospital – or decked
out at the funeral home. Look at you! You didn't even break your
glasses.
DAISY It was the car's fault.
20 BOOLIE: Mama, the car didn't just back over the driveway and land on
the Pollard's garage all by itself. You had it in the wrong gear.
DAISY: I did not!
BOOLIE: You put it in reverse instead of drive. The police report shows
that.
25 DAISY: You should have let me keep my La Salle.
BOOLIE: Your La Salle was eight years old.

▷ **1** *ignition:* Zündung **4** *thereof* (fml.): of it **6** *bristle:* (here) anger **7** *feistiness:*
(here) (aggressive) energy **8–9** *Junior Chamber of Commerce:* group of young
successful local businessmen who meet to promote their interests **16** *lay* (non-
standard AE): lie **16–17** *deck sb. out:* jdn. aufbahren **20** *driveway* (AE) = (BE)
drive: private path for vehicles leading up to a house **21** *gear:* Gang **23** *drive:* gear
position in an automatic car for driving forward **25** *La Salle:* make of car

DAISY: I don't care. It never would have behaved this way. And you know it.

BOOLIE: Mama, cars, don't behave. They are behaved upon. The fact is you, all by yourself, demolished that Packard.

DAISY: Think what you want. I know the truth. 5

BOOLIE: The truth is you shouldn't be allowed to drive a car any more.

DAISY: No.

BOOLIE: Mama, we are just going to have to hire somebody to drive you.

DAISY: No *we* are not. This is my business. 10

BOOLIE: Your insurance policy is written so that they are going to have to give you a brand new car.

DAISY: Not another Packard, I hope.

BOOLIE: Lord Almighty! Don't you see what I'm saying?

DAISY: Quit talking so ugly to your mother. 15

BOOLIE: Mama, you are seventy-two years old and you just cost the insurance company twenty-seven hundred dollars. You are a terrible risk. Nobody is going to issue you a policy after this.

DAISY: You're just saying that to be hateful.

BOOLIE: O.K. Yes. Yes I am. I'm making it all up. Every insurance 20
company in America is lined up in the driveway waving their fountain pens and falling all over themselves to get you to sign on. Everybody wants Daisy Werthan, the only woman in the history of driving to demolish a three week old Packard, a two car garage and a free standing tool shed in one fell swoop! 25

DAISY: You talk so foolish sometimes, Boolie.

BOOLIE: And even if you could get a policy somewhere, it wouldn't be safe. I'd worry all the time. Look at how many of your friends have men to drive them. Miss Ida Jacobs, Miss Ethel Hess, Aunt Nonie –

DAISY: They're all rich. 30

BOOLIE: Daddy left you plenty enough for this. I'll do the interviewing at the plant. Oscar in the freight elevator knows every colored man in Atlanta worth talking about. I'm sure in two weeks time I can find you somebody perfectly –

DAISY: No! 35

BOOLIE: You won't even have to do anything, Mama. I told you. I'll do all the interviewing, all the reference checking, all the –

DAISY: No. Now stop running your mouth! I am seventy-two years old as you so gallantly reminded me and I am a widow, but unless they

8

40 rewrote the Constitution and didn't tell me, I still have rights. And one of my rights is the right to invite who I want – not who you want – into my house. You do accept the fact that this is my house? What I do not want – and absolutely will not have is some – (*She gropes for a bad enough word.*) some chauffeur sitting in my
45 kitchen, gobbling my food, running up my phone bill. Oh, I hate all that in my house!

BOOLIE: You have Idella.

DAISY: Idella is different. She's been coming to me three times a week since you were in the eighth grade and we know how to stay out of
50 each other's way. And even so there are nicks and chips in most of my wedding china and I've seen her throw silver forks in the garbage more than once.

BOOLIE: Do you think Idella has a vendetta against your silverware?

DAISY: Stop being sassy. You know what I mean. I was brought up to
55 do for myself. On Forsyth Street we couldn't afford them and we did for ourselves. That's still the best way, if you ask me.

BOOLIE: Them! You sound like Governor Talmadge.

DAISY: Why, Boolie! What a thing to say! I'm not prejudiced! Aren't you ashamed?

60 BOOLIE: I've got to go home. Florine'll be having a fit.

DAISY: Y'all must have plans tonight.

BOOLIE: Going to the Ansleys for a dinner party.

DAISY: I see.

BOOLIE: You see what?

65 DAISY: The Ansleys. I'm sure Florine bought another new dress. This is her idea of heaven on earth, isn't it?

BOOLIE: What?

DAISY: Socializing with Episcopalians.

▷ **4** *demolish sth.:* destroy sth. · *Packard:* make of car **11** *insurance policy:* Versicherungsvertrag **25** *in one fell swoop:* in a single action **32** *plant:* factory · *freight elevator:* lift for heavy goods **37** *reference checking:* act of finding out about a person's former job or behavior **39** *gallant:* polite **44** *grope for sth.:* search for sth. in one's mind with difficulty **45** *gobble sth.:* eat sth. noisily and fast **51** *wedding china:* porcelain dishes, cups, etc. given as wedding presents **53** *vendetta:* (here) personal war **54** *sassy* (AE infml.): showing no respect **57** *Governor Talmadge = Herman E. Talmadge* (1913–2002): governor of Georgia (1948–1955), known for his support of segregation **60** *have a fit:* einen Anfall kriegen **68** *socialize with sb.:* mix with sb., e.g. at parties · *Episcopalian:* member of a church with a high social prestige

BOOLIE: You're a doodle, Mama. I guess Aunt Nonie can run you anywhere you need to go for the time being.

DAISY: I'll be fine.

BOOLIE: I'll stop by tomorrow evening.

DAISY: How do you know I'll be here? I'm certainly not dependent on you for company.

BOOLIE: Fine. I'll call first. And I still intend to interview colored men.

DAISY: No!

BOOLIE: Mama!

DAISY: (*Singing to end discussion.*)
  After the ball is over.
  After the break of morn
  After the dancers leaving
  After the stars are gone
  Many a heart is aching
  If you could read them all –

(*Lights fade on her as she sings and come up on Boolie at his desk at the Werthan Company. He sits at a desk piled with papers, and speaks into an intercom.*)

BOOLIE: O.K., Miss McClatchey. Send him on in. (*He continues working at his desk. Hoke Coleburn enters, a black man of about 60, dressed in a somewhat shiny suit and carrying a fedora, a man clearly down on his luck but anxious to keep up appearances.*) Yes, Hoke isn't it?

HOKE: Yassuh. Hoke Coleburn.

BOOLIE: Have a seat there. I've got to sign these letters. I don't want Miss McClatchey fussing at me.

HOKE: Keep right on with it. I got all the time in the worl'.

BOOLIE: I see. How long you been out of work?

HOKE: Since back befo' las' November.

BOOLIE: Long time.

HOKE: Well, Mist' Werthan, you try bein' me and looking for work. They hirin' young if they hirin' colored, an' they ain' even hirin' much young, seems like. (*Boolie is involved with his paperwork.*) Mist' Werthan? Y'all people Jewish, ain' you?

BOOLIE: Yes we are. Why do you ask?

HOKE: I'd druther drive for Jews. People always talkin' bout they stingy and they cheap, but don' say none of that 'roun' me.

BOOLIE: Good to know you feel that way. Now, tell me where you
40   worked before.

HOKE: Yassuh. That what I'm gettin' at. One time I workin' for this
       woman over near Little Five Points. What was that woman's
       name? I forget. Anyway, she president of the Ladies Auxiliary over
       yonder to the Ponce De Leon Baptist Church and seem like she
45   always bringing up God and Jesus and do unto others. You know
       what I'm talkin' bout?

BOOLIE: I'm not sure. Go on.

HOKE: Well, one day, Mist' Werthan, one day that woman say to me,
       she say "Hoke, come on back in the back wid me. I got something
50   for you." And we go on back yonder and, Lawd have mercy, she
       have all these old shirts and collars be on the bed, yellow, you
       know, and nasty like they been stuck off in a chifferobe and forgot
       about. Thass' right. And she say "Ain' they nice? They b'long to my
       daddy befo' he pass and we fixin' to sell 'em to you for twenty five
55   cent apiece."

BOOLIE: What was her name?

HOKE: Thass' what I'm thinkin'. What WAS that woman's name?
       Anyway, as I was goin' on to say, any fool see the whole bunch of
       them collars and shirts together ain' worth a nickel! Them's the
60   people das callin' Jews cheap! So I say "Yassum, I think about it"
       and I get me another job fas' as I can.

BOOLIE: Where was that?

HOKE: Mist' Harold Stone, Jewish gentleman jes' like you. Judge, live
       over yonder on Lullwater Road.

65 BOOLIE: I knew Judge Stone.

HOKE: You doan' say! He done give me this suit when he finish wid it.
       An' this necktie too.

BOOLIE: You drove for Judge Stone?

▷ **1** *doodle* (infml.): silly person **1–2** *run sb. somewhere:* drive sb. somewhere
12 *morn* (poetic): morning **19** *intercom:* Sprechanlage **23** *fedora:* type of hat
37 *druther* (non-standard): rather **38** *stingy:* unwilling to spend money · *cheap:*
having no taste or manners **43** *Ladies Auxiliary:* church charity organization run
by women **43–44** *over yonder to* (non-standard): over there at **45** *bring sth. up:*
start talking about sth. · *do unto others:* (here) reference to the Bible teaching that
one should treat other people as though they were you **52** *chifferobe:* type of
wardrobe **54** *pass = pass away:* die **54** *fix* (non-standard): intend **59** *nickel:* US
coin worth 5¢

11

HOKE: Seven years to the day nearabout. An' I be there still if he din'
die, and Miz Stone decide to close up the house and move to her
people in Savannah. And she say "Come on down to Savannah
wid me, Hoke." Cause my wife dead by then and I say "No thank
you." I didn' want to leave my grandbabies and I don' get along   5
with that Geechee trash they got down there.

BOOLIE: Judge Stone was a friend of my father's.

HOKE: You doan' mean! Oscar say you need a driver for yo' family.
What I be doin'? Runnin' yo' children to school and yo' wife to the
beauty parlor and like dat?   10

BOOLIE: I don't have any children. But tell me –

HOKE: Thass' a shame! My daughter bes' thing ever happen to me. But
you young yet: I wouldn't worry none.

BOOLIE: I won't. Thank you. Did you have a job after Judge Stone?

HOKE: I drove a milk truck for the Avondale Dairy thru the whole war   15
– the one jes' was.

BOOLIE: Hoke, what I'm looking for is somebody to drive my mother
around.

HOKE: Excuse me for askin', but how come she ain' hire fo' herself?

BOOLIE: Well, it's a delicate situation.   20

HOKE: Mmmm Hmm. She done gone 'roun' the bend a little? That'll
happen when they get on.

BOOLIE: Oh no. Nothing like that. She's all there. Too much there is
the problem. It just isn't safe for her to drive any more. She knows
it, but she won't admit it. I'll be frank with you. I'm a little   25
desperate.

HOKE: I know what you mean 'bout dat. Once I was outta work my
wife said to me "Oooooh, Hoke, you ain' gon get now nother job."
And I say "What you talkin' bout, woman?" And the very next
week I go to work for that woman in Little Five Points. Cahill! Ms.   30
Frances Cahill. And then I go to Judge Stone and they the reason I
happy to hear you Jews.

BOOLIE: Hoke, I want you to understand, my mother is a little high-
strung. She doesn't want anybody driving her. But the fact is you'd
be working for me. She can say anything she likes but she can't fire   35
you. You understand?

HOKE: Sho' I do. Don't you worry none about it. I hold on no matter
what way she run me. When I nothin' but a little boy down there

on the farm above Macon, I use to wrastle hogs to the ground at
40 killin' time, and ain' no hog get away from me yet.

BOOLIE: How does twenty dollars a week sound?

Hoke: Soun' like you got yo' Mama a chauffeur.

(Lights fade on them and come up on Daisy who enters her living
room with the morning paper. She reads with interest. Hoke enters
45 *the living room. He carries a chauffeur's cap instead of his hat.*
Daisy's concentration on the paper becomes fierce when she senses
Hoke's presence.)

Mornin', Miz Daisy.

DAISY: Good morning.

50 HOKE: Right cool in the night, wadn't it?

DAISY: I wouldn't know. I was asleep.

HOKE: Yassum. What yo' plans today?

DAISY: That's my business.

HOKE: You right about dat. Idella say we runnin' outta coffee and
55 Dutch Cleanser.

DAISY: We?

HOKE: She say we low on silver polish too.

DAISY: Thank you. I will go to the Piggly Wiggly on the trolley this
afternoon.

60 HOKE: Now, Miz Daisy, how come you doan' let me carry you?

DAISY: No thank you.

HOKE: Aint that what Mist' Werthan hire me for?

DAISY: That's his problem.

HOKE: All right den. I find something to do. I tend yo' zinnias.

65 DAISY: Leave my flower bed alone.

HOKE: Yassum. You got a nice place back beyond the garage ain' doin'
nothin' but sittin' there. I could put you in some butterbeans and
some tomatoes and even some Irish potatoes could we get some
ones with good eyes.

▷ **3** *Savannah:* city on the coast of Georgia **6** *Geechee trash* (derog.): black
people who live in Savannah **10** *beauty parlor* (AE): women's hairdressers offer-
ing a range of beauty services **21** *round the bend* (infml.): crazy **22** *get on:* get
older **33–34** *high-strung:* nervous and difficult **38** *run sb.:* (here) treat sb.
39 *Macon:* town in Georgia · *wrastle = wrestle* · *hog* (AE): pig **46** *fierce:* (here)
intense **54** *run outta sth. = run out of sth.:* not have enough of sth. **58** *trolley*
(AE): tram **60** *carry sb.:* (here) drive sb. **64** *zinnia:* type of flower **69** *eye:*
Knospenansatz

DAISY: If I want a vegetable garden, I'll plant it for myself.

HOKE: Well, I go out and set in the kitchen, then, like I been doin' all week.

DAISY: Don't talk to Idella. She has work to do.

HOKE: Nome. I jes sit there till five o'clock. 5

DAISY: That's your affair.

HOKE: Seem a shame, do. That fine Oldsmobile settin' out there in the garage. Ain't move a inch from when Mist' Werthan rode it over here from Mitchell Motors. Only got nineteen miles on it. Seem like that insurance company give you a whole new car for nothin'. 10

DAISY: That's your opinion.

HOKE: Yassum. And my other opinion is a fine rich Jewish lady like you doan b'long draggin' up the steps of no bus, luggin' no grocery store bags. I come along and carry them fo' you.

DAISY: I don't need you. I don't want you. And I don't like you saying 15 I'm rich.

HOKE: I won' say it, then.

DAISY: Is that what you and Idella talk about in the kitchen? Oh, I hate this! I hate being discussed behind my back in my own house! I was born on Forsyth Street and, believe you me, I knew the value 20 of a penny. My brother Manny brought home a white cat one day and Papa said we couldn't keep it because we couldn't afford to feed it. My sisters saved up money so I could go to school and be a teacher. We didn't have anything!

HOKE: Yassum, but look like you doin' all right now. 25

DAISY: And I've ridden the trolley with groceries plenty of times!

HOKE: Yassum, but I feel bad takin' Mist' Werthan's money for doin' nothin'. You understand? (*She cuts him off in the speech.*)

DAISY: How much does he pay you?

HOKE: That between me and him, Miz Daisy. 30

DAISY: Anything over seven dollars a week is robbery. Highway robbery!

HOKE: Specially when I doan do nothin' but set on a stool in the kitchen all day long. Tell you what, while you goin' on the trolley to the Piggly Wiggly, I hose down yo' front steps. 35

(*Daisy is putting on her hat.*)

DAISY: All right.

HOKE: All right I hose yo' steps?

DAISY: All right the Piggly Wiggly. And then home. Nowhere else.

40 HOKE: Yassum.

DAISY: Wait. You don't know how to run the Oldsmobile!

HOKE: Miz Daisy, a gear shift like a third arm to me. Anyway, thissun automatic. Any fool can run it.

DAISY: Any fool but me, apparently.

45 HOKE: Ain' no need to be so hard on yoseff now. You cain' drive but you probably do alota things I cain' do. It all work out.

DAISY: (*Calling offstage.*) I'm gone to the market, Idella.

HOKE: (*Also calling.*) And I right behind her! (*Hoke puts on his cap and helps Daisy into the car. He sits at the wheel and backs the*

50 *car down the driveway. Daisy, in the rear, is in full bristle.*) I love a new car smell. Doan' you? (*Daisy slides over to the other side of the seat.*)

DAISY: I'm nobody's fool, Hoke.

HOKE: Nome.

55 DAISY: I can see the speedometer as well as you can.

HOKE: I see dat.

DAISY: My husband taught me how to run a car.

HOKE: Yassum.

DAISY: I still remember everything he said. So don't you even think for

60 a second that you can – Wait! You're speeding! I see it!

HOKE: We ain' goin' but nineteen miles an hour.

DAISY: I like to go under the speed limit.

HOKE: Speed limit thirty five here.

DAISY: The slower you go, the more you save on gas. My husband told

65 me that.

HOKE: We barely movin'. Might as well walk to the Piggly Wiggly.

DAISY: Is this your car?

HOKE: Nome.

DAISY: Do you pay for the gas?

70 HOKE: Nome.

DAISY: All right then. My fine son may think I'm losing my abilities, but I am still in control of what goes on in my car. Where are you going?

HOKE: To the grocery store.

75 DAISY: Then why didn't you turn on Highland Avenue?

▷ **7** *Oldsmobile:* make of car **13** *drag:* (here) move with difficulty · *lug sth.:* carry sth. with difficulty **35** *hose sth. down:* clean sth. with water sprayed from a hose (= Schlauch) **42** *gear shift:* Schaltknüppel

15

HOKE: Piggly Wiggly ain' on Highland Avenue. It on Euclid, down there near –

DAISY: I know where it is and I want to go to it the way I always go. On Highland Avenue.

HOKE: That three blocks out of the way, Miz Daisy.   5

DAISY: Go back! Go back this minute!

HOKE: We in the wrong lane! I cain' jes –

DAISY: Go back I said! If you don't, I'll get out of this car and walk!

HOKE: We movin'! You cain' open the do'!

DAISY: This is wrong! Where are you taking me?   10

HOKE: The sto'.

DAISY: This is wrong. You have to go back to Highland Avenue!

HOKE: Mmmm Hmmmm.

DAISY: I've been driving to the Piggly Wiggly since the day they put it up and opened it for business. This isn't the way! Go back! Go   15
back this minute!

HOKE: Yonder the Piggly Wiggly.

DAISY: Get ready to turn now.

HOKE: Yassum.

DAISY: Look out! There's a little boy behind that shopping cart!   20

HOKE: I see dat.

DAISY: Pull in next to the blue car.

HOKE: We closer to the do' right here.

DAISY: Next to the blue car! I don't park in the sun! It fades the upholstery.   25

HOKE: Yassum. (*He pulls in, and gets out as Daisy springs out of the back seat.*)

DAISY: Wait a minute. Give me the car keys.

HOKE: Yassum.

DAISY: Stay right here by the car. And you don't have to tell everybody   30
my business.

HOKE: Nome. Doan' forget the Dutch Cleanser now. (*She fixes him with a look meant to kill and exits. Hoke waits by the car for a minute, then hurries to the phone booth at the corner.*) Hello? Miz McClatchey? Hoke Coleburn here. Can I speak to him?   35
(*Pause.*) Mornin sir, Mist' Werthan. Guess where I'm at? I'm at dishere phone booth on Euclid Avenue right next to the Piggly Wiggly. I jes drove yo' Mama to the market. (*Pause.*) She flap a little on the way. But she all right. She in the store. Uh oh. Miz

40 Daisy look out the store window and doan' see me, she liable to
throw a fit right there by the checkout. (*Pause.*) Yassuh, only took
six days. Same time it take the Lawd to make the worl'.

(*Lights out on Hoke. We hear a choir singing.*)

CHOIR: May the words of my mouth
45 And the meditations of my heart
Be acceptable in Thy sight, O Lord
My strength and my redeemer. Amen.

(*Light up on Hoke waiting by the car, looking at a newspaper.
Daisy enters in a different hat and a fur piece.*)

50 HOKE: How yo' temple this mornin', Miz Daisy?

DAISY: Why are you here?

HOKE: I bring you to de temple like you tell me. (*He is helping her
into the car.*)

DAISY: I can get myself in. Just go. (*She makes a tight little social
55 smile and a wave out the window.*) Hurry up out of here! (*Hoke
starts up the car.*)

HOKE: Yassum.

DAISY: I didn't say speed. I said get me away from here.

HOKE: Somethin' wrong back yonder?

60 DAISY: No.

HOKE: Somethin' I done?

DAISY: No. (*A beat.*) Yes.

HOKE: I ain' done nothin'!

DAISY: You had the car right in front of the front door of the temple!
65 Like I was Queen of Romania! Everybody saw you! Didn't I tell
you to wait for me in the back?

HOKE: I jes tryin' to be nice. They two other chauffeurs right behind
me.

DAISY: You made me look like a fool. A g.d. fool!

70 HOKE: Lawd knows you ain' no fool, Miz Daisy.

DAISY: Slow down. Miriam and Beulah and them, I could see what
they were thinking when we came out of services.

HOKE: What that?

▷ **24–25** *upholstery:* seat covers **38** *flap* (infml.): become angry and excited
40 *liable:* likely **41** *checkout:* Kasse **47** *redeemer:* Erlöser **49** *fur piece:* piece of
clothing made with fur (= Pelz) **50** *temple:* synagogue; also, Jewish religious
worship **62** *beat:* short pause **69** *g.d.* (abbr.) = *god damn* **71** *Beulah* ['bjuːlə]
72 *services* (AE) = (BE) *service:* ceremony of religious worship

DAISY: That I'm trying to pretend I'm rich.

HOKE: You is rich, Miz Daisy!

DAISY: No I'm not! And nobody can ever say I put on airs. On Forsyth Street we only had meat once a week. We made a meal off of grits and gravy. I taught the fifth grade at the Crew Street School! I did 5 without plenty of times, I can tell you.

HOKE: And now you doin' with. What so terrible in that?

DAISY: You! Why do I talk to you? You don't understand me.

HOKE: Nome, I don't. I truly don't. Cause if I ever was to get ahold of what you got I be shakin' it around for everybody in the world to 10 see.

DAISY: That's vulgar. Don't talk to me! (*Hoke mutters something under his breath.*) What? What did you say? I heard that!

HOKE: Miz Daisy, you needs a chauffeur and Lawd know, I needs a job. Let's jes leave it at dat. 15

(Light out on them and up on Boolie, in his shirtsleeves. He has a phone to his ear.)

BOOLIE: Good morning, Mama. What's the matter? (*Pause.*) What? Mama, you're talking so fast I … What? All right. All right. I'll come by on my way to work. I'll be there as soon as I can. 20

(Light out on him and up on Daisy, pacing around her house in a winter bathrobe. Boolie enters in a topcoat and scarf.)

I didn't expect to find you in one piece.

DAISY: I wanted you to be here when he comes. I wanted you to hear it for yourself. 25

BOOLIE: Hear what? What is going on?

DAISY: He's stealing from me!

BOOLIE: Hoke? Are you sure?

DAISY: I don't make empty accusations. I have proof!

BOOLIE: What proof? 30

DAISY: This! (*She triumphantly pulls an empty can of salmon out of her robe pocket.*) I caught him red-handed! I found this hidden in the garbage pail under some coffee grounds.

BOOLIE: You mean he stole a can of salmon?

DAISY: Here it is! Oh I knew. I knew something was funny. They all 35 take things, you know. So I counted.

BOOLIE: You counted?

DAISY: The silverware first and the linen dinner napkins and then I went into the pantry. I turned on the light and the first thing that

18

40 caught my eye was a hole behind the corned beef. And I knew right
away. There were only eight cans of salmon. I had nine. Three for
a dollar on sale.

BOOLIE: Very clever, mama. You made me miss my breakfast and be
late for a meeting at the bank for a thirty-three cent can of salmon.
45 (*He jams his hand in his pocket and pulls out some bills.*) Here!
You want thirty-three cents? Here's a dollar! Here's ten dollars!
Buy a pantry full of salmon!

DAISY: Why, Boolie! The idea! Waving money at me like I don't know
what! I don't want the money. I want my things!

50 BOOLIE: One can of salmon?

DAISY: It was mine. I bought it and I put it there and he went into my
pantry and took it and he never said a word. I leave him plenty of
food every day and I always tell him exactly what it is. They are like
having little children in the house. They want something so they
55 just take it. Not a smidgin of manners. No conscience. He'll never
admit this. "Nome," he'll say. "I doan know nothin' bout that."
And I don't like it! I don't like living this way! I have no privacy.

BOOLIE: Mama!

DAISY: Go ahead. Defend him. You always do.

60 BOOLIE: All right. I give up. You want to drive yourself again, you just
go ahead and arrange it with the insurance company. Take your
blessed trolley. Buy yourself a taxicab. Anything you want. Just
leave me out of it.

DAISY: Boolie ... (*Hoke enters in an overcoat.*)

65 HOKE: Mornin, Miz Daisy. I b'lieve it fixin' to clear up. S'cuse me, I
didn't know you was here Mist' Werthan.

BOOLIE: Hoke, I think we have to have a talk.

HOKE: Jes' a minute. Lemme put my coat away. I be right back. (*He
pulls a brown paper bag out of his overcoat.*) Oh, Miz Daisy.
70 Yestiddy when you out with yo' sister I ate a can o' your salmon. I
know you say eat the leff over pork chops, but they stiff. Here, I

▷ **3** *put on airs:* behave as though one is more important than one is **4** *off of* (AE
infml.) out of · *grits:* Maisbrei **5** *gravy:* Fleischsoße **5–6** *do without:* accept the
lack of certain things because one is poor **15** *leave it at that* (infml.): end an
argument **22** *topcoat* (AE): lightweight overcoat **31** *salmon:* Lachs **32** *catch sb.
red-handed:* discover sb. in the act of doing sth. wrong **39** *pantry:* small room next
to the kitchen for storing food **55** *smidgin* (infml.): small bit **62** *blessed* ['blesid]:
(here) damned

done buy you another can. You want me to put it in the pantry fo you?

DAISY: Yes. Thank you, Hoke.

HOKE: I'll be right wit' you Mist' Werthan. (*Hoke exits. Daisy looks at the empty can in her hand.*)   5

DAISY: (*Trying for dignity.*) I've got to get dressed now. Goodbye, son. (*She pecks his cheek and exits. Lights out on him. We hear sounds of birds twittering. Lights come up brightly, indicating hot sun. Daisy, in light dress, is kneeling, a trowel in her hand, working by a gravestone. Hoke, jacket in hand, sleeves rolled up, stands   10 nearby.*)

HOKE: I jes' thinkin', Miz Daisy. We bin out heah to the cemetery three times dis mont' already and ain' even the twentieth yet.

DAISY: It's good to come in nice weather.

HOKE: Yassum. Mist' Sig's grave mighty well tended. I b'leve you the   15 best widow in the state of Georgia.

DAISY: Boolie's always pestering me to let the staff out here tend to this plot. Perpetual care they call it.

HOKE: Doan' you do it. It right to have somebody from the family lookin' after you.   20

DAISY: I'll certainly never have that. Boolie will have me in perpetual care before I m cold.

HOKE: Come on now, Miz Daisy.

DAISY: Hoke, run back to the car and get that pot of azaleas for me and set it on Leo Bauer's grave.   25

HOKE: Miz Rose Bauer's husband?

DAISY: That's right. She asked me to bring it out here for her. She's not very good about coming. And I believe today would've been Leo's birthday.

HOKE: Yassum. Where the grave at?   30

DAISY: I'm not exactly sure. But I know it's over that way on the other side of the weeping cherry. You'll see the headstone. Bauer.

HOKE: Yassum.

DAISY: What's the matter?

HOKE: Nothin' the matter. (*He exits. She works with her trowel. In*   35 *a moment Hoke returns with flowers.*) Miz Daisy ...

DAISY: I told you it's over on the other side of the weeping cherry. It says Bauer on the headstone.

HOKE: How'd that look?

40 DAISY: What are you talking about?

HOKE: (*Deeply embarrassed.*) I'm talkin' bout I cain' read.

DAISY: What?

HOKE: I cain' read.

DAISY: That's ridiculous. Anybody can read.

45 HOKE: Nome. Not me.

DAISY: Then how come I see you looking at the paper all the time?

HOKE: That's it. Jes' lookin'. I dope out what's happening from the pictures.

DAISY: You know your letters, don't you?

50 HOKE: My ABC's? Yassum, pretty good. I jes' cain' read.

DAISY: Stop saying that. It's making me mad. If you know your letters then you can read. You just don't know you can read. I taught some of the stupidest children God ever put on the face of this earth and all of them could read enough to find a name on a tombstone. The
55 name is Bauer. Buh buh buh buh Bauer. What does that buh letter sound like?

HOKE: Sound like a B.

DAISY: Of course. Buh Bauer. Er er er ere er. BauER. That's the last part. What letter sounds like er?

60 HOKE: R?

DAISY: So the first letter is a –

HOKE: B

DAISY: And the last letter is an –

HOKE: R.

65 DAISY: B-R. B-R. Brr. Brr. Brr. It even sounds like Bauer, doesn't it?

HOKE: Sho' do Miz Daisy. Thass it?

DAISY: That's it. Now go over there like I told you in the first place and look for a headstone with a B at the beginning and an R at the end and that will be Bauer.

70 HOKE: We ain' gon' worry 'bout what come 'n the middle?

DAISY: Not right now. This will be enough for you to find it. Go on now.

HOKE: Yassum.

DAISY: And don't come back here telling me you can't do it. You can.

▷ **7** *peck:* kiss quickly **9** *trowel:* small garden tool **15** *tend sth.:* look after sth. **18** *plot:* piece of land · *perpetual:* everlasting **32** *weeping cherry:* type of tree **38** *headstone:* Grabstein **47** *dope sth. out* (AE sl.): work sth. out **54** *tombstone:* headstone

HOKE: Miz Daisy …

DAISY: What now?

HOKE: I 'preciate this, Miz Daisy.

DAISY: Don't be ridiculous! I didn't do anything. Now would you
please hurry up? I'm burning up out here. 5

(*Light goes out on them and in the dark we hear Eartha Kitt singing
"Santa Baby." Light up on Boolie. He wears a tweed jacket, red
vest, holly in his lapel. He is on the phone.*)

BOOLIE: Mama? Merry Christmas. Listen, do Florine a favor, all
right? She's having a fit and the grocery store is closed today. You 10
got a package of coconut in your pantry? Would you bring it when
you come? (*He calls offstage.*) Hey, honey! Your ambrosia's
saved! Mama's got the coconut! (*Back into the phone.*) Many
thanks. See you anon, Mama. Ho ho ho.

(*Light up on Daisy and Hoke in the car and out on Boolie. Daisy* 15
is not in a festive mood.)

HOKE: Ooooooh at them lit up decorations!

DAISY: Everybody's giving the Georgia Power Company a Merry
Christmas.

HOKE: Miz Florine's got 'em all beat with the lights. 20

DAISY: She makes an ass out of herself every year.

HOKE: (*Loving it.*) Yassum.

DAISY: She always has to go and put a wreath in every window she's
got.

HOKE: Mmm Hmmm. 25

DAISY: And that silly Santa Claus winking on the front door!

HOKE: I bet she have the biggest tree in Atlanta. Where she get 'em so
large?

DAISY: Absurd. If I had a nose like Florine I wouldn't go around
saying Merry Christmas to anybody. 30

HOKE: I enjoy Christmas at they house.

DAISY: I don't wonder. You're the only Christian in the place!

HOKE: 'Cept they got that new cook.

DAISY: Florine never could keep help. Of course it's none of my affair.

HOKE: Nome. 35

DAISY: Too much running around. The Garden Club this and the
Junior League that! As if any one of them would ever give her the
time of day! But she'd die before she'd fix a glass of ice tea for the
Temple Sisterhood!

22

40 HOKE: Yassum. You right.

DAISY: I just hope she doesn't take it in her head to sing this year. (*She imitates.*) Glo-o-o-o-o-o-o-o-o-o-o-o-o-o-o-oriaaaa! She sounds like she has a bone stuck in her throat.

HOKE: You done say a mouthful, Miz Daisy.

45 DAISY: You didn't have to come. Boolie would've run me out.

HOKE: I know that.

DAISY: Then why did you?

HOKE: That my business, Miz Daisy. (*He turns into a driveway and stops the car.*) Well, looka' there! Miz Florine done put a Rudolph

50 Reindeer in the dogwood tree.

DAISY: If her grandfather, old man Freitag, could see this! What is it you say? I bet he'd jump up out of his grave and snatch her baldheaded! (*Hoke opens the door for Daisy.*) Wait a minute. (*She takes a small package wrapped in brown paper from her*

55 *purse.*) This isn't a Christmas present.

HOKE: Nome.

DAISY: You know I don't give Christmas presents.

HOKE: I sho' do.

DAISY: I just happened to run across it this morning. Open it up.

60 HOKE: (*Unwrapping package.*) Ain' nobody ever give me a book. (*Laboriously reads the cover.*) Hand Writing Copy Book – Grade Five.

DAISY: I always taught out of these. I saved a few.

HOKE: Yassum.

65 DAISY: It's faded but it works. If you practice, you'll write nicely.

HOKE: (*Trying not to show emotion.*) Yassum.

DAISY: But you have to practice. I taught Mayor Hartsfield out of this same book.

HOKE: Thank you, Miz Daisy.

70 DAISY: It's not a Christmas present.

▷ **3** *'preciate sth.* = *appreciate sth.:* be thankful for sth. **8** *holly:* evergreen bush with red berries used for Christmas decoration · *lapel* [- '-]: Aufschlag **12** *ambrosia:* type of dessert **14** *anon* (joc./dated): soon **21** *ass* (infml.): fool **23** *wreath:* Kranz **26** *wink:* (of a light) flash on and off **37–38** *not give sb. the time of day:* not bother to speak to sb. or show interest in sb. **44** *say a mouthful:* make a correct remark **50** *dogwood tree:* type of bushy tree **52–53** *snatch sb. baldheaded:* grab hold of sb. quickly **55** *purse* (AE): handbag **59** *run across sth.:* find sth. by chance **61** *laboriously:* with effort

HOKE: Nome.

DAISY: Jews don't have any business giving Christmas presents. And you don't need to go yapping about this to Boolie and Florine.

HOKE: This strictly between you and me. (*We hear a record of "Rudolph the Red Nose Reindeer."*) They seen us. Mist' Werthan 5 done turn up the hi fi.

DAISY: I hope I don't spit up.

(*Hoke takes her arm and they walk off together as the light fades on them. Light picks up on Boolie wearing madras bermuda shorts and Lacoste shirt. He is in his late forties, waiting by the car.*) 10

BOOLIE: (*Calling.*) Come on, Hoke! Get a wiggle on! I'm supposed to tee off at the club at eleven thirty. (*Hoke enters.*)

HOKE: Jes' emptyin' the trash. Sad'dy garbage day.

BOOLIE: Where's Mama?

HOKE: She back in her room and she say go on widdout her. I think 15 she takin' on 'bout dis. (*They have gotten in the car, both in the front seat. Hoke is driving.*)

BOOLIE: That's crazy. A car is a car.

HOKE: Yassuh, but she done watch over dis machine like a chicken hawk. One day we park in front of de dry cleaner up yonder at the 20 Plaza and dis white man – look like some kind of lawyer, banker, dress up real fine – he done lay his satchel up on our hood while he open up his trunk, you know, and Lawd what he do that for, fore I could stop her, yo' Mama jump out de back do' and run that man every which way. She wicked 'bout her paint job. 25

BOOLIE: Did she tell you this new car has air conditioning?

HOKE: She say she doan' like no air cool. Say it give her the neck ache.

BOOLIE: Well, you know how Mama fought me, but it's time for a trade. She's losing equity on this car. I bet both of you will miss this old thing. 30

HOKE: Not me. Unh unh.

BOOLIE: Oh come on. You're the only one that's driven it all this time. Aren't you just a little sorry to see it go?

HOKE: It ain' goin' nowhere. I done bought it.

BOOLIE: You didn't! 35

HOKE: I already made the deal with Mist' Red Mitchell at the car place.

BOOLIE: For how much?

HOKE: Dat for him and me to know.

24

40 BOOLIE: For God's sake! Why didn't you just buy it right from Mama? You'd have saved money.

HOKE: Yo' Mama in my business enough as it is. I ain' studyin' makin' no monthly car payments to her. Dis mine the regular way.

BOOLIE: It's a good car, all right. I guess nobody knows that better
45 than you.

HOKE: Best ever come off the line. And dis new one, Miz Daisy doan' take to it, I let her ride in disheah now an' again.

BOOLIE: Mighty nice of you.

HOKE: Well, we all doin' what we can. Keep them ashes off my
50 'polstry.

(*Light out on them and up on Daisy's driveway. Daisy wearing traveling clothes and a hat, enters lugging a big heavy suitcase. She looks around anxiously, checks her watch and exits again. In a moment she returns with a full dress bag and a picnic basket. She*
55 *sets them by the suitcase, looks around, becoming more agitated, and exits again. Now she returns with a large elaborately wrapped package. Hoke enters, carrying a small suitcase.*)

DAISY: It's three after seven.

HOKE: Yassum. You say we leavin' at fifteen to eight.

60 DAISY: At the latest, I said.

HOKE: Now what bizness you got draggin' disheah out de house by yo'seff?

DAISY: Who was here to help me?

HOKE: Miz Daisy, it doan' take mo'n five minutes to load up de trunk.
65 You fixin' to break both yo' arms and yo' legs too fo' we even get outta Atlanta. You takin' on too much.

DAISY: I hate doing things at the last minute.

HOKE: What you talkin' 'bout? You ready to go fo' the las' week and half! (*He picks up the present.*)

DAISY: Don't touch that.

▷ **3** *yap about sth. to sb.* (sl.): go around and tell sb. about sth. **9** *madras:* special type of cotton cloth **11** *get a wiggle on* (sl.): hurry up **12** *tee off:* start playing golf **19–20** *chicken hawk:* bird that eats chickens **20** *dry cleaner:* shop that cleans clothes that cannot be washed **22** *satchel:* small case for carrying papers, etc. · *hood* (AE) = (BE) *bonnet:* Haube **23** *trunk* (AE) = (BE) *boot:* Kofferraum **25** *wicked:* (here) very protective · *paint job* (infml.): coat of paint on a car, etc. **29** *equity:* money value of a property **42** *study* (AE sl.): intend **46** *line:* assembly line

HOKE: Ain' it wrap pretty. Dat Mist' Walter's present?

DAISY: Yes. It's fragile. I'll hold it on the seat with me. (*Boolie enters carrying his briefcase and a small wrapped package.*) Well, you nearly missed us!

BOOLIE: I thought you were leaving at quarter of. 5

HOKE: She takin' on.

DAISY: Be still.

BOOLIE: Florine sent this for Uncle Walter. (*Daisy recoils from it.*) Well, it's not a snake, Mama. I think it's notepaper.

DAISY: How appropriate. Uncle Walter can't see! 10

BOOLIE: Maybe it's soap.

DAISY: How nice that you show such an interest in your uncle's ninetieth birthday.

BOOLIE: Don't start up, Mama. I cannot go to Mobile with you. I have to go to New York tonight for the convention. You know that. 15

DAISY: The convention starts Monday. And I know what else I know.

BOOLIE: Just leave Florine out of it. She wrote away for those tickets eight months ago.

DAISY: I'm sure *My Fair Lady* is more important than your own flesh and blood. 20

BOOLIE: Mama!

DAISY: Those Christians will be mighty impressed!

BOOLIE: I can't talk to you when you're like this. (*Daisy has climbed into the car. Boolie draws Hoke aside.*) I've got to talk to Hoke.

DAISY: They expect us for a late supper in Mobile. 25

BOOLIE: You'll be there.

DAISY: I know they'll fix crab. All that trouble!

BOOLIE: (*To Hoke.*) I don't know how you're going to stand all day in the car.

HOKE: She doan mean nothin'. She jes' worked up. 30

BOOLIE: Here's fifty dollars in case you run into trouble. Don't show it to Mama. You've got your map?

HOKE: She got it in wid her. Study every inch of the way.

BOOLIE: I'll be at the Ambassador Hotel in New York. On Park Avenue. 35

DAISY: It's seven sixteen.

BOOLIE: You should have a job on the radio announcing the time.

DAISY: I want to miss rush hour.

40 BOOLIE: Congratulate Uncle Walter for me. And kiss everybody in
Mobile.

DAISY: (*To Hoke.*) Did you have the air condition checked? I told you
to have the air condition checked!

HOKE: Yassum. I got the air condition checked but I doan' know what
45 for. You doan' never 'low me to turn it on.

DAISY: Hush up.

BOOLIE: Good bye! Good luck!

(*Light out on the car.*)

Good God!

50 (*Light out on Boolie and back up on the car. It's lunchtime. Daisy
and Hoke are both eating. Hoke eats while he drives.*)

HOKE: Idella stuff eggs good.

DAISY: You stuff yourself good. I'm going to save the rest of this for
later.

55 HOKE: Yassum.

DAISY: I was thinking about the first time I ever went to Mobile. It was
Walter's wedding, 1888.

HOKE: 1888! You weren't nothin' but a little child.

DAISY: I was twelve. We went on the train. And I was so excited. I'd
60 never been on a train, I'd never been in a wedding party and I'd
never seen the ocean. Papa said it was the Gulf of Mexico and not
the ocean, but it was all the same to me. I remember we were at a
picnic somewhere – somebody must have taken us all bathing –
and I asked Papa if it was all right to dip my hand in the water. He
65 laughed because I was so timid. And then I tasted the salt water on
my fingers. Isn't it silly to remember that?

HOKE: No sillier than most of what folks remember. You talkin' 'bout
the first time. I tell you 'bout the first time I ever leave the state of
Georgia?

70 DAISY: When was that?

HOKE: 'Bout twenty-five minutes back.

DAISY: Go on!

▷ **5** *quarter of* (AE): quarter to **6** *take on* (infml.): show that one is upset
8 *recoil from sth.:* move away from sth. **15** *convention:* conference **19** *My Fair
Lady:* musical written by Alan Jay Lerner (1956) and based on G.B. Shaw's
Pygmalion **30** *worked up:* nervous and excited **51** *stuff sth.:* fill sth. **59** *be in a
wedding party:* be one of the guests at a wedding **64** *timid:* shy **71** *Go on!:* You
don't really mean that

27

HOKE: Thass right. First time. My daughter, she married to Pullman porter on the N. C. & St. L., you know, and she all time goin' – Detroit, New York, St. Louis – talkin 'bout snow up aroun' her waist and ridin' in de subway car and I say, "Well, that very nice Tommie Lee, but I jes' doan' feel the need." So dis it, Miz Daisy, 5 and I got to tell you, Alabama ain' lookin' like much so far.

DAISY: It's nicer the other side of Montgomery.

HOKE: If you say so. Pass me up one of them peaches, please ma'am. (*She looks out the window. Suddenly she starts.*)

DAISY: Oh my God! 10

HOKE: What happen?

DAISY: That sign said Phenix City – thirty miles. We're not supposed to go to Phenix City. We're going the wrong way. Oh my God!

HOKE: Maybe you done read it wrong.

DAISY: I didn't. Stop the car! Stop the car! (*Very agitated, she* 15 *wrestles with the map on her lap.*) Here! Here! You took the wrong turn at Opelika!

HOKE: You took it with me. And you readin' the map.

DAISY: I was getting the lunch. Go on back! Oh my God!

HOKE: It ain' been thirty minutes since we turn. 20

DAISY: I'm such a fool! I didn't have any business coming in the car by myself with just you. Boolie made me! I should have come on the train. I'd be safe there. I just should have come on the train.

HOKE: Yassum. You should have.

(*Lights dim to suggest passage of time and come right back up* 25 *again. It is night now. Daisy and Hoke are somewhat slumped on the seats, Hoke driving wearily.*)

DAISY: They fixed crab for me. Minnie always fixes crab. They go to so much trouble! It's all ruined by now! Oh Lord!

HOKE: We got to pull over, Miz Daisy. 30

DAISY: Is something wrong with the car?

HOKE: Nome. I got to bixcused.

DAISY: What?

HOKE: I got to make water.

DAISY: You should have thought of that back at the Standard Oil 35 Station.

HOKE: Colored cain' use the toilet at no Standard Oil … You know dat.

28

DAISY: Well there's no time to stop. We'll be in Mobile soon. You can
wait.

HOKE: Yassum. (*He drives a minute then stops the car.*) Nome.

DAISY: I told you to wait!

HOKE: Yassum. I hear you. How you think I feel havin' to ax you when
can I make my water like I some damn dog?

DAISY: Why, Hoke! I'd be ashamed!

HOKE: I ain' no dog and I ain' no chile and I ain' jes' a back of the neck
you look at while you goin' wherever you want to go. I a man
nearly seventy-two years old and I know when my bladder full and
I gettin' out dis car and goin' off down de road like I got to do. And
I'm takin' de car key dis time. And that's de end of it. (*He leaves
the car, slamming his door and exits. Daisy sits very still in the
back seat. It's a dark country night. Crickets chirp, a dog barks.*)

DAISY: (*Angry.*) Hoke! (*She waits. No sound. Then, less angry.*)
Hoke! (*Silence. Darkness. Country sounds. Now she is
frightened.*) Hoke?

(*No answer. Light fades on her slowly and comes up on Boolie, in
his office. He speaks into his phone in answer to intercom buzz.*)

BOOLIE: Well, hell yes! Send him right on in here! (*Hoke enters.*) Isn't
it your day off? To what do I owe this honor?

HOKE: We got to talk.

BOOLIE: What is it?

HOKE: It Mist' Sinclair Harris.

BOOLIE: My cousin Sinclair?

HOKE: His wife.

BOOLIE: Jeanette?

HOKE: The one talk funny.

BOOLIE: She's from Canton, Ohio.

HOKE: Yassuh. She tryin' to hire me.

BOOLIE: What?

HOKE: She phone when she know Miz Daisy be out and she say "How
are they treating you, Hoke?" You know how she soun' like her

▷ **1–2** *Pullman porter:* (in the USA) railway employee who looks after passengers
on overnight journeys **2** *N.C. & St.L.:* name of a railway line **21** *I didn't have any
business coming:* I shouldn't have come **26** *slumped:* sitting low down as if tired
27 *weary:* tired **32** *bixcused* (non-standard) = *be excused:* (here) go to the toilet
46 *chile* (non-standard pron.): child **52** *cricket:* Grille · *chirp:* make a high-pitched
sound

nose stuff up. And I say "fine" and she say "Well, if you looking for a change you know where to call."

BOOLIE: I'll be damned!

HOKE: I thought you want to know 'bout it.

BOOLIE: I'll be God damned! 5

HOKE: Ain't she a mess? (*A beat.*) She say name yo' sal'ry.

BOOLIE: I see. And did you?

HOKE: Did I what?

BOOLIE: Name your salary?

HOKE: Now what you think I am? I ain' studyin' workin' for no trashy 10
somethin' like her.

BOOLIE: But she got you to thinking, didn't she?

HOKE: You might could say dat.

BOOLIE: Name your salary?

HOKE: Dat what she say. 15

BOOLIE: Well, how does sixty-five dollars a week sound?

HOKE: Sounds pretty good. Seventy-five sounds better.

BOOLIE: So it does. Beginning this week.

HOKE: Das mighty nice of you Mist' Werthan. I 'preciate it. Mist'
Werthan, you ever had people fightin' over you? 20

BOOLIE: No.

HOKE: Well, I tell you. It feel good.

(*Light out on them. We hear a phone ringing. Light up on Daisy's
house. It's a dark, winter morning and there is no light on in the
house. Daisy enters, wearing her coat over her bathrobe and* 25
*carrying a lit candle in a candlestick. She is up in her eighties now
and walks more carefully, but she is by no means decrepit.*)

DAISY: Hello?

(*Light up on Boolie at home, also dressed warmly.*)

BOOLIE: Mama, thank goodness! I was afraid your phone would be 30
out.

DAISY: No, but I don't have any power.

BOOLIE: Nobody does. That's why I called.

DAISY: I found some candles. It reminds me of gaslight back on Forsyth Street. Seems like we had ice storms all the time back then. 35

BOOLIE: I can't come after you because my driveway is a sheet of ice.
I'm sure yours is too.

DAISY: I'm all right, Boolie.

BOOLIE: I imagine they're working on the lines now. I'll go listen to my
car radio and call you back. Don't go anywhere.

DAISY: Really? I thought I'd take a jog around the neighborhood.

BOOLIE: You're a doodle, Mama.

DAISY: Love to Florine.

BOOLIE: Uh huh.

45 (*Light out on Boolie. Daisy talks to herself.*)

DAISY: Well, I guess that's the biggest lie I'll tell today. (*She tries to
read by the candlelight without much success. She hears the
door to outside open and close and then footsteps. She stands
alarmed.*) Who is it? (*Hoke enters carrying a paper bag and
50 wearing an overcoat and galoshes.*)

HOKE: Mornin' Miz Daisy.

DAISY: Hoke. What in the world?

HOKE: I learn to drive on ice when I deliver milk for Avondale Dairy.
Ain' much to it. I slip around a little comin' down Briarcliff, but
55 nothin' happen. Other folks bangin' into each other like they in
the funny papers, though. Oh, I stop at the 7–11. I figure yo' stove
out and Lawd knows you got to have yo' coffee in the mornin'.

DAISY: (*Touched.*) How sweet of you, Hoke. (*He sips his own
coffee.*)

60 HOKE: We ain' had good coffee 'roun' heah since Idella pass.

DAISY: You're right. I can fix her biscuits and you can fry her chicken,
but nobody can make Idella's coffee. I wonder how she did it.

HOKE: I doan' nome. Every time the Hit Parade come on TV, it put me
in mind of Idella.

65 DAISY: Yes.

HOKE: Sittin' up in de chair, her daughter say, spry as de flowers in
springtime, watchin' the Hit Parade like she done ev'ry Sad'dy the
Lawd sent and then, durin' the Lucky Strike Extra all of sudden,
she belch and she gone.

70 DAISY: Idella was lucky.

HOKE: Yassum. I 'spec she was. (*He starts to exit.*)

DAISY: Where are you going?

▷ **6** *mess:* (here) strange person **27** *by no means:* not at all · *decrepit:* weak, senile
50 *galoshes:* rubber coverings for shoes **56** *funny papers:* comics · *7–11:* name of
US chain of foodstores · stove: cooker **63** *nome:* (here) know, ma'am **63–64** *put
one in mind of sb./sth.:* remind one of sb./sth. **66** *spry:* full of life **69** *belch:* send
out gas from the stomach noisily

HOKE: Put descheah things up. Take off my overshoes.

DAISY: I didn't think you'd come today.

HOKE: What you mean? It ain' my day off, is it?

DAISY: Well, I don't know what you can do around here except keep
me company. 5

HOKE: I see can I light us a fire.

DAISY: Eat anything you want out of the ice box. It's all going to spoil
anyway.

HOKE: Yassum.

DAISY: And wipe up what you tracked onto my kitchen floor. 10

HOKE: Now Miz Daisy, what you think I am? A mess? (*This is an old
routine between them and not without affection.*)

DAISY: Yes, that's exactly what I think you are.

HOKE: All right, then. All right. (*He exits. She sits contented in her
chair. The phone rings.*) 15

DAISY: Hello?

(*Light on Boolie.*)

BOOLIE: It'll all be melted by this afternoon. They said so on the radio.
I'll be out after you as soon as I can get down the driveway.

DAISY: Stay where you are, Boolie. Hoke is here with me. 20

BOOLIE: How in the hell did he manage that?

DAISY: He's very handy. I'm fine. I don't need a thing in the world.

BOOLIE: Hello? Have I got the right number? I never heard you say
loving things about Hoke before.

DAISY: I didn't say I love him. I said he was handy. 25

BOOLIE: Uh huh.

DAISY: Honestly, Boolie. Are you trying to irritate me in the middle of
an ice storm?

(*She hangs up the phone. Light out on her. Boolie stands a moment
in wonder. Light out on him. In the dark we hear the sounds of* 30
horns blaring. A serious traffic jam. When the lights come up,
Daisy is in the car, wearing a hat. She is anxious, twisting in her
seat, looking out the window. Hoke enters.)

Well, what is it? You took so long!

HOKE: Couldn't help it. Big mess up yonder. 35

DAISY: What's the matter? I might as well not go to temple at all now!

HOKE: You cain' go to temple today, Miz Daisy.

DAISY: Why not? What in the world is the matter with you?

HOKE: Somebody done bomb the temple.

32

40 DAISY: What? Bomb the temple!

HOKE: Yassum. Dat why we stuck here so long.

DAISY: I don't believe it.

HOKE: That what the policeman tell me up yonder. Say it happen about a half hour ago.

45 DAISY: Oh no. Oh my God! Well, was anybody there? Were people hurt?

HOKE: Din' say

DAISY: Who would do that?

HOKE: You know as good as me. Always be the same ones.

50 DAISY: Well, it's a mistake. I'm sure they meant to bomb one of the conservative synagogues or the orthodox one. The temple is reform. Everybody knows that.

HOKE: It doan' matter to them people. A Jew is a Jew to them folks. Jes' like light or dark we all the same nigger.

55 DAISY: I can't believe it!

HOKE: I know jes' how you feel, Miz Daisy. Back down there above Macon on the farm – I 'bout ten or 'leven years old and one day my frien' Porter, his Daddy hangin' from a tree. And the day befo', he laughin' and pitchin' horseshoes wid us. Talkin' 'bout Porter and

60 me gon' have strong good right arms like him and den he hangin' up yonder wid his hands tie behind his back an' the flies all over him. And I seed it with my own eyes and I throw up right where I standin'. You go on and cry.

DAISY: I'm not crying.

65 HOKE: Yassum.

DAISY: The idea! Why did you tell me that?

HOKE: I doan' know. Seem like disheah mess put me in mind of it.

DAISY: Ridiculous! The temple has nothing to do with that!

HOKE: So you say.

70 DAISY: We don't even know what happened. How do you know that policeman was telling the truth?

HOKE: Now why would that policeman go and lie 'bout a thing like that?

▷ **7** *ice box* (AE): fridge **10** *track sth.:* (here) leave dirty footprints **22** *handy:* helpful, useful **31** *horn:* Hupe · *blare:* make a loud noise **51** *conservative, orthodox:* traditional Jewish religious groups **52** *reform:* liberal Jewish religious group **59** *pitch horseshoes:* play a game of throwing horseshoes around a stick **62** *throw up:* be sick, vomit

DAISY: You never get things right anyway.

HOKE: Miz Daisy, somebody done bomb that place and you know it too.

DAISY: Go on. Just go on now. I don't want to hear any more about it.

HOKE: I see if I can get us outta here and take you home. You feel 5 better at home.

DAISY: I don't feel bad.

HOKE: You de boss.

DAISY: Stop talking to me!

(*Lights fade on them. We hear the sound of applause. Boolie enters* 10 *in a fine three-piece suit, holding a large silver bowl. He is very distinguished, in his late fifties.*)

BOOLIE: Thank you, Red. And thank you all. I am deeply grateful to be chosen man of the year by the Atlanta Business Council, an honor I've seen bestowed on some mighty fine fellas and which I 15 certainly never expected to come to me. I'm afraid the loss here, (*He touches his hair.*) and the gain here, (*He touches his belly.*) have given me an air of competence I don't possess. But I'll tell you, I sure wish my father and my grandfather could see this. Seventy-two years ago they opened a little hole-in-the-wall shop 20 on Whitehall Street with one printing press. They managed to grow with Atlanta and to this day, the Werthan Company believes we want what Atlanta wants. This award proves we must be right. Thank you. (*Applause.*) One more thing. If the Jackets whup the Dawgs up in Athens Saturday afternoon, I'll be a completely 25 happy man.

(*Light out on him. Daisy enters her living room and dials the phone. She dials with some difficulty. Things have become harder for her to do.*)

DAISY: Hidey, Miss McClatchey. You always recognize my voice. 30 What a shame a wonderful girl like you never married. Miss McClatchey? Is my son in? Oh no. Please don't call him out of a sales meeting. Just give him a message. Tell him I bought the tickets for the UJA Banquet. Yes, UJA banquet honoring Martin Luther King on the seventeenth. Well, you're a sweet thing to say so. And 35 don't you worry. My cousin Tillie in Chattanooga married for the first time at fifty-seven.

(*Light dims and comes right back. Boolie has joined Daisy.*)

BOOLIE: How do you feel, Mama?

34

40 DAISY: Not a good question to ask somebody nearly ninety.

BOOLIE: Well you look fine.

DAISY: It's my ageless appeal.

BOOLIE: Miss McClatchey gave me your message.

DAISY: Florine is invited too.

45 BOOLIE: Thank you very much.

DAISY: I guess Hoke should drive us. There'll be a crowd.

BOOLIE: Mama, we have to talk about this.

DAISY: Talk about what?

BOOLIE: The feasibility of all this.

50 DAISY: Fine. You drive. I thought I was being helpful.

BOOLIE: You know I believe Martin Luther King has done some mighty fine things.

DAISY: Boolie, if you don't want to go, why don't you just come right out and say so?

55 BOOLIE: I want to go. You know how I feel about him.

DAISY: Of course, but Florine –

BOOLIE: Florine has nothing to do with it. I still have to conduct business in this town.

DAISY: I see. The Werthan Company will go out of business if you
60   attend the King dinner?

BOOLIE: Not exactly. But a lot of the men I do business with wouldn't like it. They wouldn't come right out and say so. They'd just snicker and call me Martin Luther Werthan behind my back – something like that. And I'd begin to notice that my banking
65   business wasn't being handled by the top dogs. Maybe I'd start to miss out on a few special favors, a few tips. I wouldn't hear about certain lunch meetings at the Commerce Club. Little things you can't quite put your finger on. And Jack Raphael over at Ideal Press, he's a New York Jew instead of a Georgia Jew and as long as
70   you got to deal with Jews, the really smart ones come from New

▷ **12** *distinguished:* looking elegant and successful **15** *bestow sth. on sb.* (fml.): give sth. to sb. **18** *air:* appearance **23** *award:* prize **24–25** *Jackets, Dawgs = Yellow Jackets, Bulldogs:* two university football teams **24** *whup sb.* (sl.) = *whip sb.:* beat sb. **25** *Athens:* city in Georgia **30** *hidey* (AE infml.): *hello* **34** *UJA* (abbr.): *United Jewish Appeal:* Jewish charitable organization **34–35** *Martin Luther King* (1929–1968): black preacher and Civil Rights leader **42** *appeal* (n.): attraction **49** *feasibility:* Durchführbarkeit **63** *snicker:* laugh in an unpleasant way **65** *the top dogs* (infml.): the best and most important people **68** *put one's finger on sth.* (idiom): identify sth.

35

York, don't they? So some of the boys might start throwing business to Jack instead of ole Martin Luther Werthan. I don't know. Maybe it wouldn't happen, but that's the way it works. If we don't use those seats, somebody else will and the good Doctor King will never know the difference, will he? 5

DAISY: If we don't use the seats? I'm not supposed to go either?

BOOLIE: Mama, you can do whatever you want.

DAISY: Thanks for your permission.

BOOLIE: Can I ask you something? When did you get so fired up about Martin Luther King? Time was, I'd have heard a different story. 10

DAISY: Why, Boolie! I've never been prejudiced and you know it!

BOOLIE: Okay. Why don't you ask Hoke to go to the dinner with you?

DAISY: Hoke? Don't be ridiculous. He wouldn't go.

BOOLIE: Ask him and see. (*Boolie exits. Daisy puts on an evening wrap and chiffon scarf over her hair. This is not done quickly.* 15 *She moves slowly. When she is ready, Hoke enters and helps her into the car. They ride in silence for a moment.*)

DAISY: I don't know why you still drive. You can't see.

HOKE: Yassum I can.

DAISY: You didn't see that mailbox. 20

HOKE: How you know what I didn't see?

DAISY: It nearly poked through my window. This car is all scratched up.

HOKE: Ain't no sucha thing.

DAISY: How would you know? You can't see. What a shame. It's a 25 bran' new car, too.

HOKE: You got this car two years come March.

DAISY: You forgot to turn.

HOKE: Ain' this dinner at the Biltmo'?

DAISY: You know it is. 30

HOKE: Biltmo' straight thissaway.

DAISY: You know so much.

HOKE: Yassum. I do.

DAISY: I've lived in Atlanta all my life.

HOKE: And ain' run a car in onto twenty years. (*A beat.*) 35

DAISY: Boolie said the silliest thing the other day.

HOKE: Tha' right?

DAISY: He's too old to be so foolish.

HOKE: Yassum. What did he say?

36

40 DAISY: Oh, he was talking about Martin Luther King. (*A beat.*) I guess
you know him, don't you?

HOKE: Martin Luther King? Nome.

DAISY: I was sure you did. But you've heard him preach?

HOKE: Same way as you – over the TV.

45 DAISY: I think he's wonderful.

HOKE: Yassum.

DAISY: You know, you could go see him in person any time you
wanted. (*No response.*) All you'd have to do is go over there to the
– what is it?

50 HOKE: Ebeneezer.

DAISY: Ebeneezer Baptist Church some Sunday and there he'll be.

HOKE: What you gettin' at, Miz Daisy?

DAISY: Well, it's so silly. Boolie said you wanted to go to this dinner
with me tonight. Did you tell him that?

55 HOKE: Nome.

DAISY: I didn't think so. What would be the point? You can hear him
anytime – whenever you want.

HOKE: You want the front do' or the side do' to the Biltmore?

DAISY: I think the side. Isn't it wonderful the way things are
60 changing?

HOKE: What you think I am, Miz Daisy?

DAISY: What do you mean?

HOKE: You think I some somethin' sittin' up here doan' know nothin'
bout how to do?

65 DAISY: I don't know what you're talking about.

HOKE: Invitation to disheah dinner come in the mail a mont' ago. Did
be you want me to go wid you, how come you wait till we in the car
on the way to ask me?

DAISY: What? All I said was that Boolie said you wanted to go.

70 HOKE: (*Sulking.*) Mmm-hmmm.

DAISY: You know you're welcome to come, Hoke.

HOKE: Mmmm-hmmm.

DAISY: Oh my stars. Well, aren't you a great big baby!

HOKE: Nevermind baby, next time you ask me someplace, ask me
75 regular.

▷ **2** *ole* (infml.): old   **9** *get fired up about sb./sth.*: become excited about sb./sth.
10 *Time was* (infml.): There was a time when   **15** *wrap*: coat   **22** *poke through sth.*:
(here) come through sth.   **70** *sulk*: be silent because of anger

DAISY: You don't have to carry on so much!

HOKE: Das' all. Less drop it.

DAISY: Honestly!

HOKE: Things changin', but they ain't change all dat much. (*They are at the door.*) I hep you to the do'. 5

DAISY: Thank you, Hoke. I can help myself.

(*Daisy gets herself out of the car, which takes some effort. Hoke sits still in his seat. Daisy looks at him when she is out of the car, but thinks better of what she was going to say and walks slowly towards the door. Lights out on them and up on Boolie at his* 10 *house.*)

BOOLIE: (*On the phone.*) Hello, Hoke? How are you?

HOKE: I'm tolerable, Mist' Werthan.

BOOLIE: What can I do for you this morning?

HOKE: It yo' Mama. 15

BOOLIE: What's the matter?

HOKE: She worked up.

BOOLIE: Why should today be different from any other day?

HOKE: No, this ain' the same.

DAISY: (*Offstage.*) Hoke? 20

HOKE: Yassum? (*Back to phone.*) She think she teachin' school. I'm real worried 'bout her. She ain' makin' sense.

BOOLIE: I'll be right there.

(*Lights out on Boolie. He exits. Daisy enters. She is in disarray. Her hair is not combed and her housecoat is open, the slip showing* 25 *underneath.*)

DAISY: Hoke? Hoke?

HOKE: Yassum?

DAISY: Where did you put my papers?

HOKE: Ain' no papers, Miz Daisy. 30

DAISY: My papers! I had them all corrected last night and I put them in the front so I wouldn't forget them on my way to school. What did you do with them?

HOKE: You talkin' outta yo' head.

DAISY: The children will be so disappointed if I don't give them their 35 homework back. I always give it back the next day. That's why they like me. Why aren't you helping me?

HOKE: What you want me to do, Miz Daisy?

DAISY: Give me the papers. I told you. It's all right if you moved them.
I won't be mad with you. But I've got to get to school now. I'll be
late and who will take care of my class? They'll be all alone. Oh
God! Oh Goddy! I do everything wrong.

HOKE: Set down. You about to fall and hurt yo'seff.

DAISY: It doesn't matter. I'm sorry. It's all my fault. I didn't do right. It's
so awful! Oh God!

HOKE: Now you lissen heah. Ain' nothin' awful 'cep the way you
carryin' on.

DAISY: I'm so sorry. It's all my fault. I can't find the papers and the
children are waiting.

HOKE: No they ain'. You ain' no teacher no mo'.

DAISY: It doesn't make any difference.

HOKE: Miz Daisy, ain' nothin' the matter wit' you.

DAISY: You don't know. You don't know. What's the difference?

HOKE: Your mind done took a turn this mornin' thass all.

DAISY: Go on. Just go on now.

HOKE: You snap right back if you jes' let yo'seff.

DAISY: I can't! I can't!

HOKE: You a lucky ole woman, you know dat?

DAISY: No! No! It's all a mess now. And I can't do anything about it!

HOKE: You rich, you well for your time and you got people care about
what happen to you.

DAISY: I'm being trouble. Oh God, I don't want to be trouble to
anybody.

HOKE: You want something to cry about, I take you to the state home,
show you what layin' out dere in de halls.

DAISY: Oh my God!

HOKE: An' I bet none of them take on bad as you doin'.

DAISY: I'm sorry. I'm so sorry. Those poor children in my class.

HOKE: You keep dis up, I promise, Mist' Werthan call the doctor on
you and just as sho' as you born, that doctor gon' have you in de
insane asylum fore you know what hit you. Dat de way you want it
to be? (*Daisy looks at him. She speaks in her normal voice.*)

DAISY: Hoke, do you still have that Oldsmobile?

▷ **9** *think better of sth.:* decide not to do sth. **13** *tolerable:* not too bad
24 *disarray:* disorder **25** *slip:* Unterrock **47** *carry on:* behave in a silly way
56 *snap back:* recover quickly **71** *insane asylum* (infml.): institution for mentally
disturbed people

HOKE: From when I firs' come here? Go on, Miz Daisy, that thing been in the junkyard fifteen years or more. I drivin' yo' next-to-las' car now. '63 Cadillac, runnin' fine as wine.

DAISY: You ought not to be driving anything, the way you see.

HOKE: How you know the way I see, less you lookin' outta my eyes? 5

DAISY: Hoke?

HOKE: Yassum?

DAISY: You're my best friend.

HOKE: Come on, Miz Daisy. You jes' –

DAISY: No. Really. You are. (*She takes his hand.*) 10

HOKE: Yassum.

(The light fades on them. Boolie enters. He is 65 now. He walks slowly around Daisy's living room, picking up a book here and there, examining an ashtray. He leafs through his mother's little leather phone book and puts it in his pocket. Hoke enters. He is 85. 15
He shuffles a bit and his glasses are very thick.)

HOKE: Mornin' Mist' Werthan.

BOOLIE: Well Hoke, good to see you. You didn't drive yourself out here?

HOKE: Nawsuh. I doan' drive now. My granddaughter run me out. 20

BOOLIE: My Lord, is she old enough to drive?

HOKE: Michelle thirty-seven. Teach biology at Spelman College.

BOOLIE: I never knew that.

HOKE: Yassuh.

BOOLIE: I've taken most of what I want out of the house. Is there 25
anything you'd like before the Goodwill comes?

HOKE: My place full to burstin' now.

BOOLIE: It feels funny to sell the house while Mama's still alive.

HOKE: I 'gree.

BOOLIE: But she hasn't even been inside the door for two years. I 30
know I'm doing the right thing.

HOKE: Doan' get me into it.

BOOLIE: I'm not going to say anything to her about it.

HOKE: You right there.

BOOLIE: By the way, Hoke, your check is going to keep coming every 35
week – as long as you're there to get it.

HOKE: I 'preciate that, Mist' Werthan.

BOOLIE: You can rest easy about it. I suppose you don't get out to see
Mama very much.

HOKE: It hard, not drivin'. Dat place ain' on no bus line. I goes in a
taxicab sometime.
BOOLIE: I'm sure she appreciates it.
HOKE: Some days she better than others. Who ain't?
BOOLIE: Well, we'd better get on out there. I guess you have a turkey
dinner to get to and so do I. Why don't we call your granddaughter
and tell her I'll run you home?
(*They exit and the light comes up on Daisy, 97, slowly moving
forward with a walker. She seems fragile and diminished, but still
vital. A hospital chair and a table are nearby. Boolie and Hoke join
her.*)
Happy Thanksgiving, Mama. Look who I brought. (*Boolie helps
Daisy from her walker into her chair.*)
HOKE: Mornin', Miz Daisy. (*She nods.*) You keepin' yo'seff busy?
(*Silence.*)
BOOLIE: She certainly is. She goes to jewelry making – how many
times a week is it, Mama? She makes all kinds of things. Pins and
bracelets. She's a regular Tiffanys.
HOKE: Ain't that something. (*Daisy seems faraway.*)
BOOLIE: (*Keeping things going.*) Hoke, you know I thought of you
the other morning on the Expressway. I saw an Avondale milk
truck.
HOKE: You doan' say.
BOOLIE: A big monster of a thing, must've had sixteen wheels. I
wonder how you'd have liked driving that around.
DAISY: (*Suddenly.*) Hoke came to see me, not you.
HOKE: This one of her good days.
BOOLIE: Florine says to wish you a Happy Thanksgiving. She's in
Washington, you know. (*No response.*) You remember, Mama.
She's a Republican National Committeewoman now.
DAISY: Good God! (*Hoke laughs, Boolie grins.*) Boolie!
BOOLIE: What is it, Mama?
DAISY: Go charm the nurses.

▷ **16** *shuffle:* walk without taking one's feet off the ground **26** *the Goodwill:*
charitable organization **48** *walker:* frame used as a support for walking ·
diminished: smaller than before **49** *vital:* (here) energetic and lively **57** *Tiffanys:*
famous American jewellery shop **60** *expressway:* motorway **69** *National
Committeewoman:* (in the USA) woman responsible for the organization and
funding of a political party **72** *charm sb.:* (here) flirt with sb.

41

BOOLIE: (*To Hoke.*) She wants you all to herself. (*To Daisy.*) You're a
   doodle, Mama. (*Boolie exits. Daisy dozes for a minute in her
   chair. Then she looks at Hoke.*)
DAISY: Boolie payin' you still?
HOKE: Every week.   5
DAISY: How much?
HOKE: That between me an' him, Miz Daisy.
DAISY: Highway robbery. (*She closes her eyes again. Then opens
   them.*) How are you?
HOKE: Doin' the bes' I can.   10
DAISY: Me too.
HOKE: Well, thass all there is to it, then. (*She nods, smiles. Silence.
   He sees the piece of pie on the table.*) Looka here. You ain' eat yo'
   Thanksgiving pie. (*She tries to pick up her fork. Hoke takes the
   plate and fork from her.*) Lemme hep you wid this. (*He cuts a*   15
   small piece of pie with the fork and gently feeds it to her. Then
   another as the lights fade slowly out.)

THE END

THE LANGUAGE
IN THE PLAY

The play is set in Georgia, one of the states in America's South-East, so there are elements typical of the Southerners' language. What is particularly striking (and perhaps difficult for German readers of the play) is Hoke's language. Hoke's use of Black English allows him to come alive for readers and audiences alike. Some of the most typical and maybe most unusual elements are explained below so that the language does not get in the way of the enjoyment of the play. After the explanations there is a reference list for the first few pages that might be helpful when getting into the play.

Phonetic Spelling
BEGINNINGS OF WORDS:
- First syllables and letters are often completely dropped (*'bout, 'cept* instead of *about, except*)
- The *th* in *they, them, this* often changes to a *d* (*dey, dem, dis*)
- There is sometimes an additional *a* in order to link words (*get ahold of*)

ENDINGS:
- Final consonants are often dropped (*talkin', ain', an'*)
- A *th* can change to *d* or *t* (*wid, mont*)

OTHER CHANGES:
- Vowel spellings change (*doan', cain't* instead of *don't, can't*)
- Words are linked (*lemme, alota, nome* instead of *let me, a lot of, no ma'am*)

Syntax/Grammar

VERB:

- There is often no inflection (*seem like ...* instead of *[it] seems like ...*)
- Forms of *be* are often left out (*she always bringing up*; *she president of ...*)
- The past tense is sometimes formed with *done* + infinitive (*he done give me* instead of *he gave me*)

OTHER DIFFERENCES:

- in negative sentences the double negative is often used (*don' say none of that ...; I wouldn't worry none*)
- subjects – usually pronouns – are sometimes dropped (*seem like ...*)
- *them* can be used for *those* (*the whole bunch of them collars*)

Reference list to get you started

pages 4–5

25 *yassuh:* yes, sir

28 *worl':* world

30 *since back befo' las' November:* since before last November

36 *Mist' Werthan:* Mister Werthan

35 *Y'all people:* you people

35 *ain':* aren't (or, in other cases, "isn't" or "am not")

37–38 *people always talkin' bout they stingy and they cheap:* people are always talking about how stingy and cheap they are

38 *don' say none of that 'roun' me:* they don't say any of that around me

42 *That what I'm gettin' at:* that's what I'm getting at

42 *I workin' for:* I was working for

44 *she president of:* she is/was president of

45–46 *seem like she always bringing up:* it seems as if she was always bringing up

50 *in the back wid me:* in the back with me

51 *Lawd:* Lord ...

51–52 *she have all these old shirts and collars be on the bed:* she had all ... lying on the bed

54 *Thass' right:* that's right

54 *b'long:* belong
55 *befo' he pass:* before he passed on
55 *'em:* them
60 *them collars:* those collars
60–61 *them's the people das callin' Jews:* those are the people that are calling Jews
61 *yassum:* yes, ma'am
64 *jes':* just
67 *doan':* don't
67 *he done give me:* he gave me
67 *when he finish wid it:* when he was/had finished with it
70 *nearabout:* nearly, about
70 *An' I be there still if he din' die:* And I'd still be there if he hadn't died
71 *Miz Stone:* Mrs. Stone

pages 6–7
6 *yo':* your
8 *like dat?:* like that?
11 *I wouldn't worry none:* I wouldn't worry (at all)
25 *you ain' gon get now nother job:* you aren't going to get another job
35 *sho' I do:* sure I do
48 *wadn't it?:* wasn't it
69 *set:* sit

pages 8–9
1 *nome:* no, ma'am
3 *eem a shame, do:* it seems a shame, it does
38–39 *thissun automatic:* this one is automatic
41 *yoseff* = yourself
41 *you cain' drive:* you can't drive

1
THE LANGUAGE OF THE SOUTH

There is much confusion about the term *pidgin*. The word itself comes from the Chinese pronunciation of the English word *business*. (It was a form of English used between the English and the Chinese in seaports in China and the Straits settlements in the nineteenth
5   century.) Technically, a "pidgin" is an auxiliary language, one that has no native speakers. In other words, it is a speech-system that has been formed to provide a means of communication between people who have no common language. When a "pidgin" (English, French or Portuguese) becomes the principal language of a speech community
10 – as on the slave ships – it evolves into a *creole*. Imagine two slaves who have met on a ship. The children of these pidgin-speaking slaves, who have been brought up to speak their parents' pidgin as a native language, then develop it into a creole. […] (p. 212)

When the slave ships arrived in West Africa, the need for a pidgin
15 occurred immediately. The slaves, from many different language backgrounds, had to communicate with each other and with their overseers. There is plenty of evidence that the slave masters broke up the various tribes to minimize the risk of rebellion. […] (p. 215)

By the time they left the slave ship, the Blacks would have become
20 familiar with quite a range of pidgin English. *In extremis*, as they were, there would have been every incentive to form a new speech community, the first step in the painful rebuilding of a shattered world. So pidgin English, borrowed from the sailors, became the slave lingua franca. […] (p. 216)

▷ **4** *the Straits settlements:* former British crown colony in South-East Asia, today Singapore and Malaysia **20** *in extremis* (Latin): in a desperate situation

It is a misconception to imagine that a pidgin is a debased form of speech without rules. A pidgin will always have its own way of constructing a sentence. What is different about a pidgin is that usually it dispenses with the difficult or unusual parts of the language, the parts that speakers from a great variety of language backgrounds would find strange or hard to learn [...] and this is the reason why Black English, whose distant ancestor is the English pidgin of the slave ships, has two simplifying characteristics: 30

1. The omission of verbs like *is*, as in: *You out of the game*.
2. The dropping of present-tense inflections, as in: *He fast in everything he do*. 35

Black English also has useful refinements that Standard English lacks – for instance the use of *be* to signify a stable condition in a sentence like: *some of them be big*. In Black English, *he working* means that "he is busy right now"; on the other hand, *he be working* means that "he has a steady job". (pp. 212–213) 40

The plantations of the deep South became a cradle of a new ingredient in American culture. The English of the slaves was having a decisive effect on the English of their White Anglo-Saxon masters. The Southern accent of the United States would almost certainly have been quite different without the influence of the Blacks. The 45 influence of Black English was felt in the fields (where slave and overseer would mix), in the house (where master and mistress used Plantation Creole to communicate with their house-slaves): but above all, it was found in the nursery. Up to the age of about six years, Black and White children grew up together, played together, and 50 learned together. In these crucial years of their development the Whites were often outnumbered by the Black slave children. Furthermore, all the nursing – as any reader of Southern literature knows – was done by Blacks. As early as the mid-eighteenth century it was reported that, "the better sort, in this country, particularly, 55 consign their children to the care of Negroes ..." (pp. 231–232)

As the nineteenth century unfolded, so-called "Nigger English", and later the "Negro dialect", became widely recognized among both Blacks and Whites. [...] (p. 228)

(From R. McCrum, W. Cran, R. MacNeil, *The Story of English*. Faber and Faber / BBC Publications, London, 1992; Chapter 6, pp. 212–232)

48

2
A GENTLEMAN'S AGREEMENT

St. Louis is a Northern town with Southern accents, where Jim Crow
walks a tightrope. Negroes are not segregated on streetcars and buses,
in the ballparks, or at the Municipal Opera. But in restaurants, the
public schools and movie houses, they are. Last week the delicate
5 balance, a matter of timing and tradition, was snapped. A reporter
casually asked the city's new welfare director, John J. O'Toole,
whether Negroes could be allowed to swim in all the city's public
pools. There was no law saying they couldn't, so O'Toole answered.
"If the colored people apply for admittance, my order is to admit
10 them. I am not going to be a party to an unlawful gentleman's agree-
ment."

On opening day at Fairgrounds Park, white swimmers drifted back
to the locker rooms in sullen anger when the first Negroes splashed
into the outdoor pool. Outside the pool fence, a mob of some 200
15 teen-agers collected. Police arrived in time to escort the Negroes
safely from the park. But all that afternoon fist fights blazed up; Negro
boys were chased and beaten by white gangs. In the gathering dust,
one grown-up rabble-rouser spoke out. "Want to know how to take
care of those niggers?" he shouted. "Get bricks. Smash their heads,
20 the dirty, filthy —."

Swinging baseball bats, the crowd shuffled in mounting excite-
ment. Then someone called out: "There's some niggers!"

▷ **1** *Jim Crow* (infml.): traditional discrimination against or segregation of blacks,
named after a character in a 19th century minstrel show (a popular entertainment
featuring "black-faced" whites) **2** *Negro:* term used officially for African-
Americans or blacks in the 1940s and 1950s, today considered offensive

The crowd cornered two terror-stricken Negro boys against a fence. Under a volley of fists, clubs and stones, the boys went down – but not before one of them had whipped out a knife and stabbed one 25 of his attackers. In a surge of fury, the nearest whites kicked and pummeled the two prostrate bodies, turned angrily on rescuing police with shouts of "nigger-lover."

Within an hour the crowd had swollen to more than 5,000. In the park along bustling Grand Boulevard busy teen-age gangs hunted 30 down Negroes. Others climbed into trucks and circled the park, looking for more targets. One Negro managed to seize a club from his attackers, flailed away in wall-eyed fear, with blood oozing through his shirt front. When police finally reached him, the crowd hooted with glee. "He must have a skull like a rock," said one 16-year-old. "I 35 kicked him twice in the head myself."

By 2 a.m., when hard-pressed police finally cleared the streets, ten Negroes and five whites had been hospitalized, one critically injured. Next day Mayor Joseph M. Darst ordered both outdoor pools closed, and ruled that St. Louis' pools and playgrounds would stay 40 segregated.

(From *Time*, July 4, 1949, pp. 17–18)

▷ **33** *wall-eyed* (AE): having eyes that are larger than normal

3
AWAY FROM HATE

Blacks in the South have made greater strides than in the rest of the country and are more hopeful of the future. For this historic breakthrough, blacks themselves are primarily responsible. In the face of intense white resistance, their struggle for equality was bitter,
5 costly and ultimately triumphant. But whites too have profited from the change. They have been liberated from an obsessive preoccupation with an unjust system of discrimination; they can now turn to more constructive projects.

In an attempt to forestall federal efforts to integrate the South,
10 whites used to argue that they "understood" blacks better than the Northerners did. That rationalization was partly true because the fate of blacks and whites has been entwined since the start of slavery. Even when they were most at odds, they often lived in close proximity and fraternized casually. Once the barriers of segregation came
15 down, it became apparent that whites and blacks had more in common in the South than they did in the North. "There was an understanding between the peoples," says Terry Sanford, president of Duke University. "Human relations always existed, and the other side was made up of people, not just an unknown mass."

(From "Race relations in the South", *Time*, Sept. 27, 1976, p. 50)

4
"WE HAVE MEMORIES IN COMMON"

Welty: [...] You share many things. I've had letters from people – I had a letter from a black friend of mine when something had happened to me, and she said, "I don't know if you remember me, but my mother was your mother's wash-lady, and I used to come to your house on the express wagon" – this would have been when we children were six or   5
seven years old – "and we used to play together." It was when my mother died; she had seen it in the paper. And she said, "She was a nice lady and you were a nice little girl. And my daughter and I think of you." She said she was now the wife of a professor at a college somewhere, but she often thought of those days. Now this was   10
completely spontaneous on her part. But that's what you remember. She shared something when she read that about my mother. She thought, "We have memories in common."

(From "Growing up in the South", in Louis D. Rubin Jr. (ed.), *The American South: Portrait of a Culture*. Voice of America Forum Series, 1979, p. 88)

▷ **1** *Welty* = *Eudora Welty* (1909–2001): famous writer from Mississippi **5** *express wagon:* type of train

5
SEGREGATION REMEMBERED

"Like most black Americans, my roots are in the South." So writes
Time Atlanta correspondent Jack White, 30, who reported on many
of the stories in this issue before taking nine months' leave for a
Nieman Fellowship at Harvard. Here is White's personal account of
5   being brought up under segregation:

My father's father was born a slave somewhere near Savannah, Ga.
My mother's father was the son of a white undertaker and his mulatto
concubine in a small town in North Carolina.

Like many other blacks, my parents migrated North to find educa-
10 tion and better opportunities. My father went to Harvard University
medical school, and my mother went to Howard's nursing school. My
parents wanted to shelter their children from segregation and all its
belittling aspects, so they settled in Washington, which turned out to
be as segregated a town as one could find.

15 In the 1950s, a clerk in a department store refused to let me sip
from a water fountain, despite my mother's plea that "he's just a little
boy." Later, when my family got its first television set, I was entranced
by the ads for Glen Echo amusement park. My mother couldn't really
explain why she couldn't take me there. The reason, of course, was
20 that Glen Echo did not admit blacks. Nor did many restaurants,
movie theaters and other public facilities.

▷ **7** *undertaker:* person who prepares dead people for burial, etc. **8** *concubine*
(old-fashioned): mistress, girlfriend **13** *belittle sb./sth.:* make sb./sth. appear
unimportant **17** *entrance sb.* [in'træns; BE -'trɑːns]: fill sb. with wonder or delight

My deepest realization of what the Old South was really like came in about 1962, when my father, brother, a friend and I drove South to my grandmother's house in Stuart, Fla. On the way we were denied a room in a Holiday Inn in Savannah, and wound up sleeping in a 25 "rooming house" (read whorehouse) that hadn't had an overnight guest in years. In Stuart, my father went into a hardware store to buy a Thermos bottle. The white clerk asked my dad, a distinguished professor of surgery at least 20 years his senior, "What you want, boy?" My father struggled to maintain his dignity as he told the clerk 30 what he wanted. I felt in my gut, for the first time, how hard it had been for black men to preserve their self-respect under a rigid system of white supremacy.

(From "Race relations in the South", *Time*, Sept. 27, 1976)

▷ **25** *wind – wou¬d – wound up:* end up **26** *read* … (infml.): by which … is meant

6
JEWS IN THE SOUTH

The South had relatively few Jews – certainly not enough to constitute
a Jewish problem under any rational view of the case. But fears and
hates often clothe themselves in old forms. And the Jew, of course,
was a butt and a scapegoat as old as Christianity. All the protests of
5 scholars have been quite unavailing to erase from the popular mind,
in the South as elsewhere, the notion that it was the Jew who crucified
Jesus. And in addition there was the consideration I have already
suggested: the Jew, with his universal refusal to be assimilated, is
everywhere the eternal Alien; and in the South, where any difference
10 had always stood out with great vividness, he was especially so.
Hence it was perfectly natural that, in the general withdrawal upon
the old heritage, the rising insistence on conformity to it, he should
come in for renewed denunciations; should, as he passed in the
street, stand in the eyes of the people as a sort of evil harbinger and
15 incarnation of all the menaces they feared and hated – external and
internal, real and imaginary.

(From W. J. Cash, *The Mind of the South*, Vintage Books, Alfred
A. Knopf, New York, 1969, p. 342)

▷ **9** *Alien:* outsider, foreigner **14** *harbinger* ['hɑːbɪndʒə] (literary): person or sign
that comes before an event to warn of it

THE AUTHOR

Alfred Uhry grew up in Atlanta, Georgia, before moving to New York to start his career in the theater. He worked first as a lyric writer for musicals, his most recent being *Parade*. In 1987 his first play *Driving Miss Daisy* opened in New York. It was awarded the Pulitzer Prize for Drama in 1988 and the film version received the Academy Award for Best Picture in 1989; Alfred Uhry himself received the Academy Award for Best Screenplay Based on Material from Another Medium. Other films he has worked on include *Mystic Pizza* and *Rich in Love*. His second play, *The Last Night of Ballyhoo*, won the 1997 Tony Award, making him the only playwright to have won the three most prestigious prizes – the Pulitzer, the Tony and the Academy Award.